MW00712859

HISTORY & GEOGRAPHY 610

Development Of Our World

LIFEPAC Test is located in the center of the booklet. Please remove before starting the unit.

Author:
Chelsea Naugle

Editor-in-chief:
Richard W. Wheeler, M.A.Ed.

Editor:
Elizabeth Loeks Bouman

Consulting Editor:
Howard Stitt, Th.M., Ed.D.

Revision Editor:
Alan Christopherson, M.S.

MEDIA CREDITS:
Page 9 (clockwise from top left): © starekase, iStock, Thinkstock; © Jorisvo, iStock, Thinkstock; © miroslavmisiura, iStock, Thinkstock; © anandoart. iStock, Thinkstock; © Dan Breckwoldt, iStock, Thinkstock; **22 (clockwise from left):** © Snowshill, iStock, Thinkstock; © Shaiith, iStock, Thinkstock; © Olga Topp, Dreamstime; **35:** © Ian Jeffery, iStock, Thinkstock; **37:** © Photos.com, Thinkstock.

Alpha Omega
PUBLICATIONS

804 N. 2nd Ave. E.
Rock Rapids, IA 51246-1759

Development Of Our World

Introduction

The development of our world has been a chain of related events. Civilization began and grew in the Fertile Crescent. Man gained knowledge. Civilizations grew. Each civilization sought to influence its world. The Greek and Roman empires developed. The modern nations of Eastern and Western Europe grew from these two empires. The modern countries of South America and Africa have grown and developed. Some of this growth has been a result of European influence. We will review some of the events and changes in our world beginning with the Cradle of Civilization.

Objectives

Read these objectives. The objectives tell you what you will be able to do when you have successfully completed this LIFEPAC®. When you have finished this LIFEPAC, you should be able to:

1. List the geographical factors that affected the development of the Fertile Crescent and the Greek and Roman empires.

2. List accomplishments of the people of the Fertile Crescent and the Greek and Roman empires.

3. Describe government, way of life, and religion of the Fertile Crescent, Greece, Rome, and the Middle Ages.

4. List effects of the Renaissance and the Industrial Revolution.

5. Give dates, causes, and results of World War I and World War II.

6. Identify the beliefs of communism.

7. Name the countries of South America and Africa.

8. Describe European influence and today's government of South American and African countries.

9. List resources of South American and African countries.

Survey the LIFEPAC. Ask yourself some questions about this study and write your questions here.

_____

_____

_____

_____

_____

_____

_____

_____

_____

_____

_____

_____

_____

_____

_____

_____

_____

_____

1. CRADLE OF CIVILIZATION

Geographical factors affect the development of a region. Several geographical factors contributed to the development and growth of the Fertile Crescent. These geographical factors were rich soil, warm climate, and sufficient water.

The Fertile Crescent was a region which stretched from the valleys of the Tigris and Euphrates Rivers and along the eastern coast of the Mediterranean Sea. The Fertile Crescent continued to the valley of the Nile River. The Fertile Crescent is also known as the Cradle of Civilization. Early civilization began and spread from this region.

The Fertile Crescent was home to a number of early civilizations. In this section of the LIFEPAC, we will be studying three: Mesopotamia, Egypt, and Israel.

Section Objectives

Review these objectives. When you have completed this section, you should be able to:

1. List the geographical factors that affected the development of the Fertile Crescent.
2. List accomplishments of the people of the Fertile Crescent.
3. Describe government, way of life, and religion of the Fertile Crescent.

Vocabulary

Study this word to enhance your learning success in this section.

bondage (bon' dij). Slavery; lack of freedom.

Note: *All vocabulary words in this LIFEPAC appear in* **boldface** *print the first time they are used. If you are not sure of the meaning when you are reading, study the definitions given.*

Pronunciation Key: hat, āge, cãre, fär; let, ēqual, tėrm; it, īce; hot, ōpen, ôrder; oil; out; cup, put, rüle; child; long; thin; /ᴛʜ/ for then; /zh/ for measure; /u/ represents /a/ in about, /e/ in taken, /i/ in pencil, /o/ in lemon, and /u/ in circus.

MESOPOTAMIA

Mesopotamia was located in the area between the Tigris and Euphrates rivers. From 3100 B.C. to 400 B.C., Mesopotamia thrived as a center of civilization.

Government. Many different tribes lived in Mesopotamia. Among them were the ancestors of the Hebrews, God's chosen people. Many battles and wars were fought between the people of Mesopotamia. Ruling empires changed often as a more powerful people conquered the existing government. Each empire was ruled by a king. Names of the various empires included Sumer, Babylonia, Assyria, Chaldea, and Persia. Abraham received his promise of land and a nation of people from God. God commanded Abraham to leave Mesopotamia and journey to Canaan, which we now know as Israel. You can read about God's command and promise in Genesis 12:1–5.

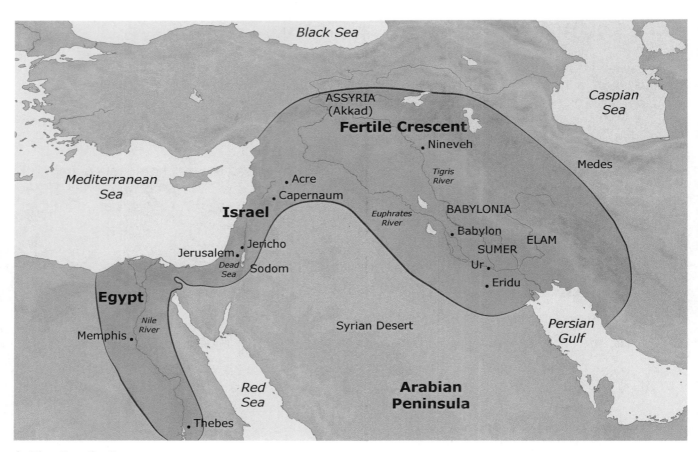

| The Fertile Crescent

 Match these items.

1.1 _____ Fertile Crescent

1.2 _____ Cradle of Civilization

1.3 _____ Mesopotamia, Israel, Egypt

1.4 _____ geographical factors of Fertile Crescent

1.5 _____ Tigris and Euphrates river valleys

1.6 _____ Hebrews

1.7 _____ Sumer, Babylonia, Assyria, Chaldea, Persia

1.8 _____ 3100 B.C. to 400 B.C.

a. population areas of Fertile Crescent

b. God's chosen people

c. region stretching from Tigris- Euphrates rivers to Nile River

d. another name for Fertile Crescent

e. eastern coast of the Mediterranean Sea

f. period during which Mesopotamia thrived

g. rich soil, warm climate, sufficient water

h. different ruling empires of Mesopotamia

i. location of Mesopotamia

Way of life. Because of the rich soil in Mesopotamia, farming was verysuccessful. Crops grew well. Food consisted of fruits, vegetables, meat, and fish. The wealthy class of citizens found time to study, to learn, and to develop art. Sculpture, pottery, and temple decorations were very beautiful.

Religion. The people of Mesopotamia believed in many gods. Beautiful temples were built to honor the gods. Religious festivals were also held to honor the many gods. The Hebrews, however, worshiped the one true God.

Accomplishments. The people of Mesopotamia accomplished many things. Education was very important. Each empire developed its own written language. Multiplication and division were used in mathematics. Improvements to help in farming were developed. Mesopotamians used a wheel. A plow with a metal tip was developed. Crops could be cultivated better and faster. Shadufs were also used to lift water. Good roads were built.

Other accomplishments included the weaving of cloth and the use of weights and measures. Trade was also important in Mesopotamia.

Write true or false.

1.9 _____ Crops grew well in Mesopotamia.

1.10 _____ Art was highly developed.

1.11 _____ Everyone farmed and no time was given to other developments.

1.12 _____ The Fertile Crescent is called the Cradle of Civilization because early civilization began and grew in this region.

1.13 _____ The people of Mesopotamia worshiped the God of the Hebrew people.

1.14 _____ The people of Mesopotamia worshiped many gods.

Complete the following activity.

1.15 List five accomplishments of the Mesopotamian people.

a. _____

b. _____

c. _____

d. _____

e. _____

EGYPT

Egypt is located in the northeastern part of Africa. The early civilization of Egypt was located along the Nile River. Egypt thrived between 2700 B.C. and 1100 B.C.

Government. The Egyptian empire was ruled by Pharaohs. A Pharaoh was all-powerful. The common people were used as labor. They built pyramids, temples for the gods, and palaces for the Pharaoh.

Way of life. The Egyptians traded with the outside world. The wealthy enjoyed many luxuries. The common people were farmers and laborers. God's children lived as slaves in Egypt for many years. The story of their **bondage** and journey to freedom is found in the book of Exodus.

Religion. The Egyptians worshiped many gods. Pyramids were built as burial places for rulers. One of the Pharaohs did introduce the worship of only one god into Egypt. This one god, however, was not the one true God. Pharaoh's answer to Moses in Exodus 5:2 shows the Egyptians did not worship God. Their god was a god of their own creation. "And Pharaoh said, Who is the Lord, that I should obey his voice to let Israel go? I know not the Lord, neither will I let Israel go."

Accomplishments. Egypt enjoyed many accomplishments. Architecture was improved. Beautiful palaces, pyramids, sphinxes, and tombs were built. Large blocks of stone were used. This building was quite an accomplishment because the Egyptians had no complex machinery like we have today.

Complete the following sentences.

1.16 Egypt is located in the northeastern part of _____ .

1.17 Civilization in Egypt grew along the _____ .

1.18 An Egyptian ruler was called a _____ .

1.19 Egyptian rulers were buried in _____ .

1.20 Beautiful palaces, pyramids, sphinxes, and tombs are examples of Egyptian

_____ .

1.21 Egyptians built large buildings of _____ .

1.22 Common people were used as farmers and _____ .

1.23 Egypt also traded with the _____ .

Answer the following question.

1.24 Do you think Egyptians who worshiped one god were more spiritual than those Egyptians

who had worshiped many gods? a. _____

Why or why not? b. _____

_____

_____

ISRAEL

Israel is a small country located along the eastern coast of the Mediterranean Sea. In ancient times it was called Canaan. God promised this land to Abraham and his descendants. The Hebrews, or the Israelites, established their kingdom here during the period of 1200 B.C. to 587 B.C.

Government. Israel had many kings through the years. Israel lost its independence in 63 B.C. The Hebrews did not regain control of Israel again until 1948.

Today, Israel is governed by a body of representatives. This group is called the Knesset. Israel also has a prime minister.

Religion. The Hebrew people were God's chosen people. He gave His Word through the Hebrew people. The Israelites lived among people who worshiped many different gods. The Hebrews worshiped the one true God.

Accomplishments. Through the Hebrews, we have received the books of the Old Testament. Other Hebrew literature includes beautiful psalms, other poetry, and the history of ancient times.

Clockwise from top left:
The Sphinx;
Moses & The Ten Commandments;
a Shaduf;
a farmer plowing a field with oxen;
the pyramids.

| Accomplishments and Contributions from the People of the Fertile Crescent

Write the letter of the correct answer on each line.

1.25 Israel is located on the eastern coast of the _____ .
   a. Mediterranean Sea   b. Persian Gulf   c. Tigris River

1.26 In ancient times, Israel was called _____ .
   a. Mesopotamia   b. Canaan   c. Egypt

1.27 Israel was the land which God promised to _____ .
   a. Abraham   b. Egypt   c. Adam

1.28 Through the Hebrews we have received the books of the _____ .
   a. church   b. Bible   c. Old Testament

1.29 Hebrew literature also gives us history of _____ .
   a. modern times   b. ancient times   c. Mediterranean Sea

1.30 Israel did not become a nation again until _____ .
   a. 63 B.C.   b. 1979   c. 1948

Review the material in this section in preparation for the Self Test. The Self Test will check your mastery of this particular section. The items missed on this Self Test will indicate specific areas where restudy is needed for mastery.

SELF TEST 1

Write true or false (each answer, 2 points).

1.01 _____ The Fertile Crescent had sufficient water.

1.02 _____ Soil was poor in the Fertile Crescent.

1.03 _____ The Fertile Crescent had a warm climate.

1.04 _____ The Fertile Crescent was an agricultural region.

1.05 _____ Mesopotamia was located along the Nile River.

1.06 _____ Many tribes, including the Hebrews, lived in Mesopotamia.

1.07 _____ Ruling empires changed often in Mesopotamia.

1.08 _____ One of the Mesopotamian empires was Canaan.

1.09 _____ The Hebrews were God's chosen people.

1.010 _____ An Egyptian ruler was called a Pharaoh.

Write the letter of the correct answer on each line (each answer, 2 points).

1.011 Egypt is located in the northeastern part of _____ .
a. the Fertile Crescent b. Africa c. the Cradle of Civilization

1.012 The Mesopotamians used a _____ to lift water.
a. *shaduf* b. pulley c. bucket

1.013 Mesopotamia was located along the _____ .
a. Nile River b. Mediterranean Sea c. Tigris-Euphrates rivers

1.014 God promised land and a nation of people to _____ .
a. Canaan b. Abraham c. Pharaoh

1.015 One accomplishment of the Mesopotamians was the use of the _____ .
a. wheel b. horse c. soil

1.016 Egyptian rulers were buried in _____ .
a. urns b. pyramids c. cemeteries

1.017 One Pharaoh began the worship of _____ .
a. many gods b. the true God c. one god

1.018 Through the Hebrews we have received the books of the _____ .
a. synagogue b. Temple c. Old Testament

1.019 In ancient times, Israel was called _____ .
   a. Hebrew   b. Egypt   c. Canaan

1.020 The ancestors of the Hebrews lived in _____ .
   a. Mesopotamia   b. Egypt   c. Canaan

Complete these sentences (each answer, 3 points).

1.021 From 1200 B.C. to 587 B.C. Israel was ruled by _____ .

1.022 Civilization in Egypt grew along the _____ .

1.023 Israel is located on the eastern coast of _____ .

1.024 The Egyptians used large _____ in their building.

1.025 The common people of Egypt were used as farmers and _____ .

1.026 Among their accomplishments, the Mesopotamians also wove _____ .

1.027 The Mesopotamians had a written _____ .

1.028 The people of Mesopotamia worshiped _____ .

1.029 The Mesopotamians used a plow with a _____ .

1.030 Most Egyptians worshiped _____ .

Match these items (each answer, 2 points).

1.031 _____ Mesopotamia, Israel, Egypt

1.032 _____ Cradle of Civilization

1.033 _____ Fertile Crescent

1.034 _____ Sumer, Babylonia, Assyria, Chaldea, Persia

1.035 _____ geographical factors of the Fertile Crescent

1.036 _____ weights and measures, multiplication and division

1.037 _____ pyramids, palaces, tombs, sphinxes

1.038 _____ 1948

1.039 _____ God of the Hebrew people

1.040 _____ trade

a. Mediterranean Sea

b. the one true God

c. accomplishments of the Mesopotamian people

d. population areas of Fertile Crescent

e. examples of Egyptian architecture

f. ruling empires of Mesopotamia

g. important activity in Mesopotamia and Egypt

h. another name for Fertile Crescent

i. warm climate, rich soil, sufficient water

j. Israel became a nation again

k. region stretching from Tigris-Euphrates rivers to Nile River

Answer these questions (each answer, 5 points).

1.041   Why is the Fertile Crescent called the Cradle of Civilization? _____

_____

_____

1.042   How was the religion of the Hebrew people different from the religion of the people

of Mesopotamia and Egypt?_____

_____

_____

| 80 / 100 | SCORE _____ | TEACHER _____ _____ |
| | | initials   date |

2. GREECE, ROME, AND THE MIDDLE AGES

Two other great civilizations grew up along the Mediterranean Sea. The Greek Empire and the Roman Empire were both prosperous and powerful. Each suffered decline and then conquest.

A period of no growth and no learning followed the fall of Rome. This period was called the Middle Ages.

Section Objectives

Review these objectives. When you have completed this section, you should be able to:

1. List the geographical factors that affected the development of the Greek and Roman empires.

2. List accomplishments of the people of the Greek and Roman empires.

3. Describe the government, way of life, and religion of Greece, Rome, and the Middle Ages.

Vocabulary

Study these words to enhance your learning success in this section.

barbaric (bär bar' ik). Uncivilized.

discipline (dis' u plin). Training.

isolation (ī su lā' shun). Separation.

status (stat' us). The position or rank of someone when compared with other people.

topography (tu pog' ru fē). The physical features of the land.

triumvirate (trī um' vur it). A government led by three persons.

Pronunciation Key: hat, āge, cãre, fär; let, ēqual, tėrm; it, īce; hot, ōpen, ôrder; oil; out; cup, put, rüle; child; long; thin; /ŦH/ for then; /zh/ for measure; /u/ represents /a/ in about, /e/ in taken, /i/ in pencil, /o/ in lemon, and /u/ in circus.

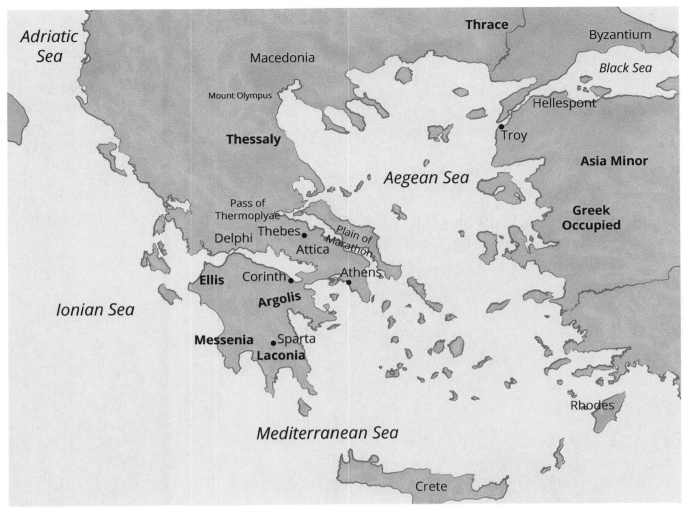

| City-states of Greece

EMPIRE OF GREECE

Greece is the lower part of the Balkan peninsula, which is located in the northeastern part of the Mediterranean Sea. Numerous islands are located along the coastline of this peninsula.

Geography. Two geographical factors influenced the development of early Greece. Greece has many good, natural harbors. These harbors allowed the early Greeks to become prosperous traders. The **topography** of Greece is rugged. Mountain ranges and deep valleys divide Greece into isolated regions. This **isolation** caused city-states to develop in early

Greece. The citizens of a city-state identified with the city-state. National identity and loyalty was not strong.

Way of life. Some common characteristics, however, created unity among the city-states. All Greeks worshiped many gods. All Greeks spoke the same language and had the same literature. The Olympic Games were also celebrated by all Greeks.

Each city-state was separate and somewhat different from the other city-states. Sparta was a Greek city-state. Sparta was known for its military **discipline**. Spartan boys were trained for service in the army at an early age. They were also trained to have first loyalty to Sparta.

Athens was another city-state. Athens became the most highly civilized and democratic city-state in Greece. Many rights were given to all classes of citizens. A noble could own only a limited amount of land. Citizens had the right to secretly vote another citizen out of society if that citizen neglected his duty or became too powerful. Athens united the other city-states into a league for protection. Athens became the strongest and most influential city-state in the league. This period was called the Golden Age of Greece.

The history of Greece is marked with wars. Some wars were fought with Persia. These wars united the Greek city-states. The city-states helped each other and defeated Persia. The Peloponnesian War was fought between Athens and Sparta. This war brought an end to the Golden Age of Greece. Sparta defeated Athens and became the leading city-state. Other Greek city-states were dissatisfied with the unjust government of Sparta. Sparta was finally conquered by other city-states. These wars among the city-states weakened the empire of Greece. Greece was then conquered.

 Write the letter of the correct answer on each line.

2.1 Greece became a trading nation because of its _____ .
   a. ships
   b. harbors
   c. mountains

2.2 City-states grew in Greece because _____ .
   a. mountains and valleys separated regions
   b. Greeks could not get along with each other
   c. Greece had no king

2.3 Greece is located in the northeastern part of_____ .
   a. the Balkan peninsula
   b. Persia
   c. the Mediterranean Sea

2.4 Sparta was known for its _____ .
   a. democratic government
   b. military discipline
   c. traders

2.5 The most highly civilized city-state in Greece was _____ .
   a. Sparta
   b. Thebes
   c. Athens

2.6 In Athens all citizens had many _____ .
   a. votes
   b. rights
   c. weapons

2.7 All Greek city-states were united into a league during the _____ .

a. Olympic Games

b. Peloponnesian War

c. Golden Age of Greece

Answer the following questions.

2.8 What effect did the Peloponnesian War have on the empire of Greece?

_____

_____

_____

2.9 Name three things which all Greeks had in common.

a. _____

b. _____

c. _____

Contributions. We have examples in our world today of accomplishments from the civilization of Greece.

Many buildings today are examples of Greek architecture. Three styles of columns were used in Greek architecture. Many buildings today use a Greek-style column.

Science has been influenced by the civilization of Greece. Greece established a large library and the first school for scientific learning. Euclid wrote a book on geometry. Eratosthenes wrote a book on geography using lines of latitude and longitude. Pythagoras wrote advanced theories in mathematics which we still use today.

Greek doctors began using the Hippocratic oath. The oath stated they would practice with honesty. Medical doctors today still take that oath. Some medical instruments used today are the kinds of instruments used by Greek doctors.

Greece made many contributions in government. Greece introduced democratic methods. The United States has used some of these ideas in its government. The right of a trial by jury came from the Greeks.

The Greek civilization also helped to spread Christianity. The Greek language was used to write the New Testament. The Greek language was spoken in many areas of the world because Greece dominated much of the world.

Decline. After the Golden Age of Greece, the civilization began to decline. The democratic methods were not used in government. Other areas such as living conditions and spiritual growth also began to decline. Rome began to dominate the Mediterranean world. In 146 B.C. Greece became part of the Roman Empire.

Complete the following sentences.

2.10 We see examples of Greek architecture in _____ today.

2.11 In architecture today we see examples of the three kinds of Greek _____ .

2.12 Euclid wrote a book on _____ .

2.13 Eratosthenes wrote a book on geography using lines of _____ .

2.14 Pythagoras wrote advanced theories in _____ .

2.15 Medical doctors today still take the _____ .

2.16 Medical doctors still use some of the same kinds of _____ .

2.17 From the Greeks came the right of a trial _____ .

2.18 The New Testament was written in _____ .

2.19 At its decline, Greece became a part of the _____ .

EMPIRE OF ROME

The Roman Empire became the controlling influence in the Mediterranean world after the fall of the Greek Empire. The Romans contributed much to their own world and to our world today.

Geography. Geography influenced the development of the Roman Empire. Two mountain ranges protected Rome from large-scale invasions. The mountain ranges were the Apennine Mountains to the east and the Alps to the north. Rome was a large city located on seven steep, wooded hills with a plain below. The plain was fertile and farmers grew many crops. Enemy tribes could attack the plain; however, Rome developed a strong military force to defend itself against the neighboring tribes. Rome's military strength also allowed Rome to conquer the neighboring tribes. Rome then gained control of the peninsula of Italy.

Government. Rome gained control of Italy. Other countries became a threat to Rome's security. Rome used its military strength to conquer other lands and enlarge its empire.

The Punic Wars were fought between Rome and Carthage for many years.

Carthage was located in North Africa. Rome defeated Carthage. Carthage became a Roman province. Rome ruled the entire Mediterranean world by 133 B.C.

From 133 B.C. to 27 B.C., a period of unrest existed in Rome. Farmers, slaves, and common people were very dissatisfied with the government of Rome. The ruling class was small. Rulers did not give rights to other citizens. For a while Rome allowed three men to rule at the same time. These rulers were called a **triumvirate**. This form of government did not work. The three men could not work together. They became rivals instead.

In 27 B.C. Augustus Caesar became the first emperor of Rome. Augustus Caesar ruled well. His rule began a peaceful time for the Roman Empire. After his death, the Roman Empire continued to prosper. Gradually, over a period of years, the great empire of Rome began to decline.

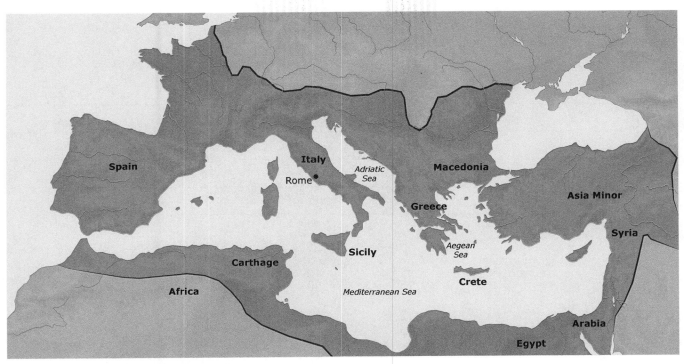

| The Roman Empire in A.D. 180

Write true or false.

2.20 _____ Rome is located on the Balkan peninsula.

2.21 _____ The Alps and the Apennines made it difficult for enemies to mount large-scale invasions on Rome from the north and the east.

2.22 _____ Rome was built on seven hills with a fertile plain below.

2.23 _____ Rome developed military strength to defend itself against enemy tribes.

2.24 _____ After gaining control of Italy, Rome fought the Mediterranean Wars.

2.25 _____ Carthage became a Roman province.

2.26 _____ Rome controlled the entire Mediterranean world.

2.27 _____ Rome had no unrest at home.

2.28 _____ A triumvirate was a government by four persons.

2.29 _____ The triumvirate form of government did not work well.

2.30 _____ Augustus Caesar was the first Roman dictator.

2.31 _____ The Roman empire lasted peacefully for two hundred years.

Complete the following activity.

2.32 Rewrite each false statement in 2.20–2.31 so that it is a true statement.

a. _____

b. _____

c. _____

d. _____

e. _____

Way of life. Four classes of people lived in Rome. The aristocrats were the upper class. This class was small, but had much **status**. The aristocrats were the ruling class. The equestrians were the next class. The equestrian class consisted of the merchants and bankers. The common citizens were the farmers and industrial workers. The lowest class was made up of the slaves.

Most Romans worshiped many gods. Some of the very poor became Christians. Christ's teachings offered an escape from a cruel life. Christianity spread throughout the whole Roman Empire. The Roman rulers were threatened by Christ and His teachings.

For this reason, Christians were severely persecuted in Rome. The rulers did not understand that Christ had come to establish a heavenly kingdom. They feared He had plans to establish an earthly kingdom. The Roman rulers feared that Christ would take over the Roman Empire. Jesus had no plans to take over the Roman Empire. In John 18:36 we read, "Jesus answered, My kingdom is not of this world: if my kingdom were of this world, then would my servants fight, that I should not be delivered to the Jews: but now is my kingdom not from hence."

Contributions. The Romans accomplished much. They influenced our world today through their accomplishments.

The Romans were builders. They built good roads, bridges, and aqueducts. The disciples used these roads as they journeyed to spread the teachings of Christ. Rome still uses some of the ancient aqueducts.

Latin was the language in which the Romans wrote. Latin became the basis for the Spanish, French, and Italian languages. Some English words are derived from Latin. Many medical and scientific terms come from Latin.

The Romans influenced the profession of law. One of the Roman beliefs which we follow today is the right of private ownership. Another Roman belief is the right to be considered innocent until proven guilty.

Match the following items.

2.33	_____	aristocrats
2.34	_____	equestrians
2.35	_____	common citizens
2.36	_____	slaves
2.37	_____	Christianity
2.38	_____	good road system
2.39	_____	aqueducts
2.40	_____	Latin
2.41	_____	right to be considered innocent until proven guilty

a. lowest class of people in Rome

b. still in use today

c. threat to Roman rulers

d. ruling class in Rome

e. worship of many gods

f. used by disciples to spread Christ's teachings

g. merchants and bankers

h. Roman contribution to law

i. language which became the basis for Spanish, French, and Italian

j. farmers and industrial workers

Decline. Many factors caused the fall of the Roman Empire. Dishonesty and violence were part of life in Rome. Trade and the value of money decreased. Laws took away people's freedom to choose jobs. Soil became overworked. Farmers could not grow plentiful crops.

Fierce tribes from the north invaded Rome. The Roman Empire was conquered by these tribes. A period known as the Dark Ages and the Middle Ages began.

Complete the following activity.

2.42 List five factors that caused the fall of the Roman Empire.

a. _____

b. _____

c. _____

d. _____

e. _____

Answer the following question.

2.43 What was the period following the conquest of Rome called?

_____

DARK AGES IN THE MIDDLE AGES

The **barbaric** tribes north of the Roman Empire conquered Rome. These tribes did not come from a civilization as advanced and educated as Rome. Life was different under the rule of these fierce tribes. This period from A.D. 395 to A.D. 1500 is known as the Middle Ages. The first five hundred years of the Middle Ages were so bad they are called the Dark Ages.

The feudal system. Many wars were fought during the Dark Ages. Men fought for power and land. Many powerful men gained control of areas of land. These men became the kings of their land. The way in which the land was distributed was known as the feudal system.

Each king had a loyal group of lords and nobles who fought for him. Each noble was given land called a manor. The manor had its own pasture lands, mill, wine press, church, and village. Both kings and nobles lived in large castles.

Each noble gave land to vassals. The vassals performed certain duties for the noble. Villeins were a lower class of people than vassals. Villeins lived in the village. Villeins were required to work for the noble each day. Serfs were the lowest class of people. A serf could not leave the manor without permission. The noble provided food and housing for the serf. Like a slave, the serf was owned by the noble and worked as a servant.

Way of life. Life was difficult for all classes of people during the Middle Ages. Few schools existed, and learning was at a standstill. Health and sanitation practices were very primitive.

| Life in the Middle Ages

The Middle Ages was a time of violence and wars. Castles were built for protection. Kings fought against kings. Nobles fought against nobles. Everyone wanted to gain more land.

Few people could read. Few books were available.

Sanitation and health practices were primitive. Garbage was usually thrown in the streets. Dirt floors and streets were common. Water became contaminated. Disease and plagues killed many people. People of the Middle Ages did not know enough about medicine to cure most illnesses.

Toward the end of the Middle Ages, people began to pass laws to improve sanitation and health. A law was passed that required the sick to remain isolated from other citizens. Another law forbade citizens to throw garbage in the streets. While yet another law forbade citizens from polluting water with dyes.

 Complete the following activities.

2.44 Use the following words to write a description of the feudal system.

| king | manor | noble | vassal |
| villein | village | serf | castle |

_____

_____

_____

_____

_____

_____

_____

2.45 Use an encyclopedia or other resources to find out where some castles are still located today. List five castles and their locations.

_____

_____

_____

_____

_____

TEACHER CHECK _____ _____

initials   date

2.46 After reading about the way of life during the Middle Ages, tell why you think part of this period was called the Dark Ages.

_____

_____

_____

_____

_____

_____

_____

_____

_____

2.47 Unscramble these letters to make words which describe health and sanitation problems during the Middle Ages.

a. braagge _____

b. seadeis _____

c. treaw _____

Education. The barbaric tribes destroyed schools and books when they conquered the Roman Empire.

Only a few books existed during the Dark Ages in the Middle Ages. These books were handwritten by monks. These monks were known as scribes. Scribes spent long hours copying the Bible. They also copied other religious literature. They wrote records of the events of their day. The Latin language was used. Latin was understood by all European scholars.

Gradually, schools began to grow. The Catholic Church established the first schools to teach prayers and music to the choir boys.

The monks began to teach other subjects such as grammar, numbers, gardening, and philosophy. Girls attended school in nunneries. Nuns taught such subjects as cooking, needlework, music, and care of the sick.

Larger schools and even universities were formed. People began to take an interest in learning. Two rulers did much to provide the opportunity for all to learn. These rulers were King Alfred of the Danes in England and Charlemagne in France.

With the growth of schools, the world began to emerge from the Dark Ages.

✎ Place an *X* beside each statement which describes education during the Dark Ages in the Middle Ages.

2.48 _____ Few books existed.

2.49 _____ Many schools were in every city.

2.50 _____ Monks copied books by hand.

2.51 _____ The Catholic Church established the first school.

2.52 _____ Monks taught grammar, numbers, and philosophy.

2.53 _____ Girls attended the same schools as boys.

2.54 _____ Nuns taught cooking, needlework, and music.

2.55 _____ Charlemagne and King Alfred were against learning.

2.56 _____ Growth of schools helped to bring an end to the Dark Ages.

Crusades and cathedrals. During the Middle Ages, people were very religious. Faith in God and the Catholic Church were important to everyone. Large, beautiful cathedrals were built of stone. Each cathedral had many beautiful stained glass windows. Many of these cathedrals still stand in Europe today. People gave time, labor, and money to the church.

People also joined crusades. Crusaders journeyed to the Holy Land in an effort to win it back from the Muslims. Only the First Crusade experienced any success. Being unsuccessful did not stop other crusades from being made. They all met with defeat. Crusaders had enthusiasm and a goal. They did not, however, conquer the Muslims. Crusaders did bring back new ideas, new merchandise, and new religious views.

Trade system. The Crusades affected the growth of trade and towns. Merchandise from foreign lands was brought back from the Crusades. A powerful merchant class grew.

People were eager to buy the silk, perfumes, dyes, and jewels. Merchants built more and larger shops to meet this demand. Merchants became a wealthy class of citizens. Some merchants became wealthy enough to buy land from nobles. The first villages grew up around the castles. As trade grew, the villages and towns grew.

Merchants who sold the same kind of merchandise built shops together on the same street. Guilds were formed. Each guild set up rules and prices for products and services. Guilds also provided training and experience for young men who wished to join a trade.

The Crusades, interest in learning, and prosperity of merchants and townspeople began to bring an end to the Middle Ages. People became interested in traveling and exploring. The new period which followed the Dark Ages and the Middle Ages is known as the Renaissance.

Write true or false.

2.57 _____ Faith in God was very important to the people of the Middle Ages.

2.58 _____ We have only pictures of the beautiful cathedrals built during the Middle Ages.

2.59 _____ The Crusades had more economic effects than spiritual effects.

2.60 _____ Towns and trade grew as a result of merchandise from the crusades.

2.61 _____ Merchandise brought back from the crusades included jewels, silk, perfume, and dyes.

2.62 _____ Merchants formed guilds.

2.63 _____ Guilds did not accept new members.

2.64 _____ The period following the Middle Ages is known as the Renaissance.

Complete the following activity.

2.65 List the three things which helped to bring an end to the Middle Ages.

    a. _____

    b. _____

    c. _____

Review the material in this section in preparation for the Self Test. This Self Test will check your mastery of this particular section as well as your knowledge of the previous section.

SELF TEST 2

Write true or false (each answer, 2 points).

2.01 _____ Greece became a trading empire because of her good harbors.

2.02 _____ Mountain ranges and deep valleys divide Greece into isolated regions.

2.03 _____ During the Golden Age of Greece, the city-states were united into a league.

2.04 _____ Three population areas of the Fertile Crescent were Greece, Egypt, and Mesopotamia.

2.05 _____ Two Greek city-states were Athens and Sparta.

2.06 _____ The Greek Empire was weakened by wars with foreign countries.

2.07 _____ All Greek people worshiped many gods, spoke the same language, had the same literature, and celebrated the Olympic Games.

2.08 _____ Greece introduced democratic methods in government and the idea of a trial by jury.

2.09 _____ God promised land and a nation of people to Abraham.

2.010 _____ The New Testament was written in Latin.

Write the letter of the correct answer on each line (each answer, 2 points).

2.011 Medical doctors today still take the oath originated by Greek doctors called the _____ .
a. Hippocratic oath b. Pharmaceutical oath c. Democratic oath

2.012 In architecture today, we see examples of the three styles of Greek _____ .
a. windows b. arches c. columns

2.013 Crops grew in the Fertile Crescent because of a warm climate, rich soil, and _____ .
a. sufficient water b. much land c. good trade routes

2.014 For a while, Rome was governed by a _____ .
a. triumvirate b. president c. counsel

2.015 To defend itself, Rome developed _____ .
a. military strength b. large forts c. a trade system

2.016 The first emperor of Rome was _____ .
a. Alexander the Great b. Charlemagne c. Augustus Caesar

2.017 Four classes of people in Rome were slaves, common citizens, equestrians, and _____ .
a. emperors b. aristocrats c. aqueducts

2.018   The language which became the basis for Spanish, French, and Italian is _____ .
  a. Greek   b. Hebrew   c. Latin

2.019   Many poor people in the Roman Empire became _____ .
  a. Christians   b. wealthy   c. merchants

2.020   The period following the conquest of Rome is called the _____ .
  a. Greek Empire   b. Renaissance   c. Middle Ages

Complete these sentences (each answer, 3 points).

2.021   The land given to a noble was called a _____ .

2.022   Both kings and nobles lived in large _____ .

2.023   Villeins were required to work for the noble each day but were allowed to live in the

  _____ .

2.024   A serf was like a _____ .

2.025   During the Middle Ages, as a result of garbage and dirt left in the streets, three health and

  sanitation problems that arose were contaminated water, disease, and _____ .

2.026   During the Middle Ages, monks copied _____ by hand.

2.027   During the Middle Ages, the first school was established by the _____ .

2.028   During the Middle Ages, there were few books and other literature, and _____ .

2.029   The Hebrew people worshiped _____ .

2.030   The region stretching from the Tigris and Euphrates rivers to the Nile River was called the

  _____ .

Match these items (each answer, 2 points).

2.031 _____ feudal system

2.032 _____ cathedrals

2.033 _____ guilds

2.034 _____ crusades

2.035 _____ merchants

2.036 _____ Renaissance

2.037 _____ plow with metal tip

2.038 _____ Cradle of Civilization

2.039 _____ Hebrew people

2.040 _____ jewels, perfume, silk

a. groups formed by merchants

b. period following Middle Ages

c. merchandise from crusades

d. system of land distribution during Middle Ages

e. God's chosen people

f. vassal

g. journeys made to Holy Land

h. another name for Fertile Crescent

i. wealthy class of people which grew after the crusades

j. large, beautiful churches built during Middle Ages

k. agricultural development from Mesopotamia

Answer these questions (each answer, 5 points).

2.041 Why were the first five hundred years after the fall of Rome called the Dark Ages?

_____

_____

_____

_____

_____

_____

2.042 What are three reasons the Middle Ages came to an end?

a. _____

b. _____

c. _____

80/100

SCORE _____ TEACHER _____ _____

initials   date

3. MODERN NATIONS OF EUROPE

Europe is divided into Western Europe and Eastern Europe. Each has developed differently. Western Europe experienced a Renaissance or rebirth following the Middle Ages. Exploration and colonization resulted. Western Europe has also experienced an Industrial Revolution and two World Wars. You will review the effects of the Renaissance, the Industrial Revolution, and the World Wars. Eastern Europe has developed a different form of government. You will review the beliefs of communism.

Section Objectives

Review these objectives. When you have completed this section, you should be able to:

4. List effects of the Renaissance and the Industrial Revolution.

5. Give dates, causes, and results of World War I and World War II.

6. Identify beliefs of communism.

Vocabulary

Study these words to enhance your learning success in this section.

alliance (u lī′ uns). An agreement between two or more countries, groups, or people to work together in doing something.

corrupt (ku rupt′). Dishonest.

strait (strāt). A narrow channel between two larger bodies of water.

wages (wāj′ es). Payment for labor performed.

Pronunciation Key: hat, āge, cãre, fär; let, ēqual, tėrm; it, īce; hot, ōpen, ôrder; oil; out; cup, put, rüle; child; long; thin; /ᵺ/ for then; /zh/ for measure; /u/ represents /a/ in about, /e/ in taken, /i/ in pencil, /o/ in lemon, and /u/ in circus.

HISTORY & GEOGRAPHY 610

LIFEPAC TEST

NAME _____

DATE _____

SCORE _____

$$\frac{80}{100}$$

HISTORY & GEOGRAPHY 610: LIFEPAC TEST

Write true or false (each answer, 2 points).

1. _____ Germany was divided between the United States and England following World War II.

2. _____ The city of Berlin was not divided following World War II.

3. _____ Today, all of Germany is a democracy.

4. _____ Most of the people of the Fertile Crescent worshiped many gods.

5. _____ The Fertile Crescent is also known as the Cradle of Civilization.

6. _____ Greece was ruled by city-states because regions were divided and isolated by mountain ranges and deep valleys.

7. _____ Crusades were journeys made to the Holy Land during the Middle Ages.

8. _____ The Industrial Revolution brought changes to the government of England.

9. _____ World War II began in 1939.

10. _____ Modern nations of Eastern Europe have a communist form of government.

Write the letter of the correct answer on each line (each answer, 2 points).

11. Three population areas of the Fertile Crescent were Egypt, Israel, and _____ .
    a. Greece   b. Mesopotamia   c. Sudan

12. The New Testament was written in the _____ language.
    a. Greek   b. Latin   c. Hebrew

13. Land distribution during the Middle Ages was called _____ .
    a. feudal system   b. manor   c. real estate

14. Kings and nobles lived in large _____ .
    a. villages   b. serfs   c. castles

15. During the Dark Ages and the Middle Ages there were _____ .
    a. many books and schools   b. few books and schools   c. few wars

16. During the Middle Ages many beautiful _____ were built.
    a. cathedrals   b. pyramids   c. temples

17. The period of awakening following the Middle Ages is known as the _____ .
    a. feudal system   b. Dark Ages   c. Renaissance

18. World War I began in _____ .
a. 1914   b. 1948   c. 1876

19. Three sources of energy during the Industrial Revolution were coal, steam, and _____ .
a. water power   b. electric power   c. horse power

20. Western European countries have influenced the development of most countries in _____ .
a. Eastern Europe   b. Africa   c. Asia

Complete these lists (each numbered problem, 10 points).

21. List seven resources from South America.

a. _____   b. _____

c. _____   d. _____

e. _____   f. _____

g. _____

22. What two things does Africa need to prosper?

a. _____   b. _____

Match these items (each answer, 2 points).

23. _____ weights and measures, wheel, plow with metal tip

24. _____ garbage, contaminated water, disease

25. _____ pyramids, tombs, and sphinxes

26. _____ classless society, business and industry belong to government, state is all important

27. _____ silk, perfume, jewels

28. _____ aqueducts, good roads, right to private ownership, assumed innocent until proved guilty

29. _____ Martin Luther, John Knox, John Calvin

30. _____ Magna Carta

31. _____ democratic methods of government, trial by jury

32. _____ United Nations

a. merchandise from crusades

b. Renaissance document which gave more freedom to all people

c. contributions of Greek Empire

d. accomplishments of Mesopotamian people

e. built by Egyptians

f. Protestants who worked for reforming the church

g. organization formed after World War II

h. causes of World War I

i. contributions of Roman Empire

j. beliefs of communism

k. health and sanitation problems during the Middle Ages

Answer these questions (each numbered problem, 10 points).

33. What geographical factors influenced the development of the Fertile Crescent?

    _____

    _____

    _____

34. What were two of the positive effects and two of the negative effects that the Industrial Revolution had on life?

    Positive

    a. _____

    b. _____

    Negative

    c. _____

    d. _____

WESTERN EUROPE

In this section you will study the development of the modern nations of Europe. You will first look at the development of the countries in Western Europe. You will then look at the development of the countries of Eastern Europe.

Renaissance. Renaissance means rebirth. After the Dark Ages and the Middle Ages, the countries of Western Europe experienced a rebirth or awakening. This awakening occurred in learning, art, exploration, religion, and other fields.

Many schools were established. People were taught to think for themselves. This freedom to think for oneself was the foundation for America's freedom of thought and worship.

During the Renaissance, explorers sought westerly trade routes by water to India and the Orient. Christopher Columbus was one of these explorers. He discovered the Bahamas. He thought he had found the islands off the coast of India. After Columbus many other explorers sailed westward. Colonies were established in North America and South America by Portugal, Spain, England, and Italy. Other explorers discovered water routes to India. In 1497 Vasco da Gama found a water route to India. He sailed around the southern tip of Africa. In 1519 Ferdinand Magellan sailed westward from Portugal. His fleet of five ships sailed through a **strait** in southern South America and on to the Philippine Islands. Only one shipload of sailors

| A map of Europe

survived the voyage to return to Portugal. This voyage was the first voyage around the world.

The Roman Catholic Church had grown very strong during the Middle Ages. Faith in God and the church was very important to the rich and the poor. Many good people served in the church. Some clergy, however, had **corrupted** the practices of the church. During the Renaissance some men encouraged new freedom in religion for all men.

A Catholic priest named Martin Luther left the Roman Catholic Church. His followers are called Lutherans. Luther believed each individual could approach God for forgiveness and salvation. He encouraged people to read the Scriptures for themselves. Luther's teachings brought a spiritual awakening in Europe. The awakening led to reformation or the reforming of the church.

Luther and others like him protested the corrupt practices of the church. For this reason they were called Protestants. Another Protestant was John Calvin. Calvin founded the Reformed Church. John Knox was also a Protestant. He formed the Presbyterian Church.

Match the following items.

3.1	_____	Renaissance
3.2	_____	Columbus
3.3	_____	Vasco da Gama
3.4	_____	Magellan
3.5	_____	Martin Luther
3.6	_____	Protestants
3.7	_____	John Calvin
3.8	_____	John Knox
3.9	_____	reformation

a. first voyage around the world

b. Roman Catholic priest who left the church

c. rebirth, awakening

d. people who protested corrupt practices of the church

e. reforming of the church

f. founded Reformed Church

g. Philippine Islands

h. discovered Bahamas

i. discovered water route to India by sailing south of Africa

j. founded Presbyterian Church

Complete the following activity.

3.10 List three things which Martin Luther believed an individual could do for himself spiritually.

a. _____

b. _____

c. _____

Answer the following question.

3.11 What effect did the new freedom in learning have on the way of life in America today?

_____

_____

_____

New freedom and awakening occurred in other areas of life. King John of England signed the Magna Carta. The Magna Carta was a document which guaranteed certain rights and privileges to all people. The Magna Carta was the first step by the people to obtain more freedom in government. The belief grew that all men were equal. People also believed man had the right and ability to govern themselves.

 Complete the following sentences.

3.12 King John of England signed the _____ .

3.13 This document guaranteed certain rights and privileges to _____ .

3.14 The Magna Carta led the way for more _____ .

3.15 All men are created _____ .

3.16 Men have the right and ability to _____ .

Industrial Revolution. The Renaissance, or rebirth, ended in Europe at the close of the sixteenth century. The next one hundred years brought steady growth in Western Europe. Portugal, Spain, France, and England established colonies in North and South America. World trade was important.

The beginning of the eighteenth century brought a new age to Western Europe. This age brought many changes to industry. The new age also brought many changes to the people of Western Europe. It was called the Industrial Revolution.

People in the colonies were a growing market for European goods and services. The colonies also supplied more raw materials to the factories. Trade between Western Europe and the colonies was brisk.

New power sources and new inventions allowed industry to expand. With new power, industry could manufacture more products for trade. New energy sources were coal, steam, and electric power. Coal was used as a fuel for blast furnaces. Blast furnaces were used in factories which manufactured iron products. A steam-powered engine made large changes in the textile industries. The discovery of steam power led to many inventions. Steamboats and steam locomotives were used for transporting people and goods. Factories could manufacture goods more quickly with electric power.

Write the letter of the correct answer on each line.

3.17 The Renaissance was followed by a quiet period in Western Europe of _____ .
    a. no growth   b. colonization and trade   c. less freedom

3.18 The Industrial Revolution began in the _____ .
    a. eighteenth century   b. twentieth century   c. sixteenth century

3.19 The Industrial Revolution brought changes to _____ .
    a. religion   b. government   c. industry

3.20 The colonies supplied _____ .
    a. raw materials   b. slave labor   c. ships

3.21 During this period, trading was very _____ .
    a. slow   b. active   c. unimportant

3.22 Manufacturing of iron products changed with the discovery of _____ .
    a. steam   b. coal   c. steel

3.23 Steam power brought changes to the textile industry and _____ .
    a. wool   b. cotton   c. transportation

3.24 Another source of energy used in the Industrial Revolution was _____ .
    a. electric power   b. water power   c. charcoal power

Five countries were affected the most by the changes and growth in industry. These countries were France, Germany, Belgium, the United States, and England. England, however, became the center of the Industrial Revolution in Western Europe.

In many ways, the Industrial Revolution brought a better way of life to England. People could buy more good products at a lower cost. Factories created jobs for people. Trade increased.

The Industrial Revolution also brought some negative effects to the way of life. Factories were built on farmland. Much of England's rural life was destroyed. Cities grew and became dirty and crowded. Coal from factories added

soot and dirt to the air. People continued to move to the cities to be near the jobs. Factory workers had to work long hours. Even children were employed. Some children died from being overworked. Labor unions were eventually formed to protect children and adult workers from abuse.

Long hours, difficult work, bad working conditions, and dirty, crowded living conditions in the cities were some of the negative effects of the Industrial Revolution in England.

John and Charles Wesley were brothers. They brought Christ's teachings to the people of England. John Wesley traveled all over England teaching the people of God's love. He told of the need to have a personal relationship with

| Industrial Revolution

Jesus Christ. Charles Wesley wrote beautiful hymns which are still sung today. Through these two brothers, many people became Christians. Christianity gave these people strength and hope for their lives. Some Christians worked to improve conditions.

Sunday schools were begun in England to teach reading, writing, and the principles of religion. Children worked in the factories six days a week, therefore, the schools were held on Sundays. Laws were soon passed and children went to school and did not work. Sunday schools continued to teach them principles of religion on Sundays.

Write true or false.

3.25 _____ England was the center of the Industrial Revolution in Western Europe.

3.26 _____ Prices of products increased as a result of the Industrial Revolution.

3.27 _____ Cities were dirty and overcrowded.

3.28 _____ Adults and children worked in factories.

3.29 _____ Working conditions were good in the factories.

3.30 _____ Labor unions were formed during the Industrial Revolution.

3.31 _____ John and Charles Wesley were cousins.

3.32 _____ The Wesleys brought Christ's teachings to the people of England.

3.33 _____ Sunday schools were begun to teach children reading, writing, and religion on Sunday because they worked six days a week.

Age of unrest. An age of unrest in Western Europe followed the Industrial Revolution. This period was marked by two world wars.

Disputes over boundaries and territory were the main causes of World War I. Tensions existed between countries. Competition existed over control of foreign countries and bases. Western European countries each wanted to control and own more land. Two **alliances** were formed among Western European countries. The Triple Entente was formed between France, Great Britain, and Russia. The Triple Alliance was formed between Germany, Austria-Hungary, and Italy.

World War I began June 28, 1914. Archduke Francis Ferdinand of Austria-Hungary and his wife were assassinated by a Serbian student. Austria-Hungary declared war on Serbia.

Germany entered the war because of its alliance with Austria-Hungary. Slowly, other countries joined the conflict. Austria-Hungary and its allies became known as the Central Powers. The countries opposing the Central Powers were called the Allied Powers. The United States was among the Allied Powers.

The war ended November 11, 1918. The armistice was signed. The Allied Powers had defeated the Central Powers. Total responsibility for World War I was placed on Germany. One-eighth of Germany's territory was taken. Other Central Power countries were reduced in size, as well.

Write the letter of the correct answer on each line.

3.34 Tension between countries existed because countries wanted more _____ .
a. money   b. territory   c. freedom

3.35 France, Great Britain, and Russia formed the _____ .
a. Triple Entente   b. Triple Alliance   c. Central Powers

3.36 Germany, Austria-Hungary, and Italy formed the _____ .
a. Triple Entente   b. Triple Alliance   c. Allied Powers

3.37 World War I began in _____ .
a. 1918   b. 1948   c. 1914

3.38 The armistice was signed in _____ .
a. 1918   b. 1948   c. 1914

3.39 The United States fought with the _____ .
a. Allied Powers   b. Central Powers   c. Armistice

3.40 Total responsibility for World War I was placed on _____ .
a. Austria-Hungary   b. Serbia   c. Germany

3.41 As a result of World War I, Germany and the Central Powers were reduced in _____ .
a. size   b. armies   c. money

Political problems, economic depression, and the rise of dictatorships in Western Europe led to World War II. Economic depression occurred in the United States and in Western Europe in the 1930s. Jobs and money were scarce. Food was scarce. Dictatorships grew in some countries. Adolf Hitler and the Nazis became powerful in Germany. Benito Mussolini and the Fascists gained control of Italy. First Lenin, then Stalin and the Communists, took control of Russia. Japan was ruled by an emperor and a warrior class. These dictators promised hope and economic success to people who had no hope or money. Each dictatorship sought to gain control of more land and territory.

World War II began in September, 1939. Germany invaded Poland. France and Great Britain then declared war on Germany. Germany then recruited the aid of five other European countries. Germany and its allies were known as the Axis Powers. Great Britain and her allies were called the Allied Powers. The United States supported the Allied Powers with money and supplies. Then Japan attacked the United States fleet at Pearl Harbor on December 7, 1941. The United States declared war on Japan. The United States then joined in actual combat in World War II. World War II ended in Europe with Germany's surrender on May 8, 1945.

Japan surrendered on August 10, 1945. Germany was divided into four sections. A section each was given to France, Great Britain, the United States, and Russia. The three parts given to France, Great Britain, and the United States were allowed to govern themselves. These sections were West Germany. Russia made its section part of its Communist Bloc. It was East Germany.

Berlin, the capital city of Germany, was also divided in the same way. The city of Berlin was divided by a high wall, called the Berlin Wall, with barbed wire and armed guards. The communist government put the fence and guards in place. The guards were supposed to prevent people from leaving East Berlin.

In 1989 changes began throughout Eastern Europe. East Germany allowed its people to cross the Wall. Then, it was torn down. The two Germanys agreed to reunite and on December 20, 1990, an all-German election was held. Germany is now a Federal Republic. Helmut Kohl was the first Chancellor of reunited Germany.

The United Nations was formed after World War II. Delegates from all over the world meet together. The delegates discuss political, money, health, and agricultural problems of the world.

| German invasion of Poland, World War II, September, 1939

Complete the following lists.

3.42 List three causes of World War II.

    a. _____

    b. _____

    c. _____

3.43 List three dictators of Western Europe and their countries.

    a. _____

    b. _____

    c. _____

Answer the following questions.

3.44 What event brought the United States into World War II?

_____

3.45 How were Germany and Berlin divided following World War II?

_____

_____

_____

_____

_____

_____

3.46 What important organization was formed following World War II?

_____

EASTERN EUROPE

The countries of Eastern Europe experienced a different development than that of Western Europe. Two ways in which this development differed were religion and government.

The church of early Eastern Europe. The Roman Catholic Church was the primary church for Christians in the first millennium. In 1054 the Roman Catholic Church split into two branches. The Roman Catholic Church was centered in Rome and the people of Western Europe remained a part of this church. The Eastern Orthodox Church was centered in Constantinople and primarily served the people of Eastern Europe. Eastern Orthodox Christians were persecuted under communist rule. Many priests were imprisoned or killed for proclaiming the gospel. The communist leaders in the Soviet Union wanted to create a nation free of religion.

Communism and its beliefs. Communism became the type of government in most of the countries of Eastern Europe from about 1945-1989. Communism differs from democracy. One belief of communism is that society should have no classes. Everyone should have the same status. All business, industry, control of money, and distribution of wealth should belong to the government. People in a democracy believe in free enterprise and personal freedom.

Communism did not encourage religion in a person's life. The state was all important. A loyal communist had to devote all his time and energy to the state. Most people were allowed to attend church. They could not, however, also belong to the Communist Party. Children were taught in school that there was no God. In a democracy, people enjoy a freedom to worship God.

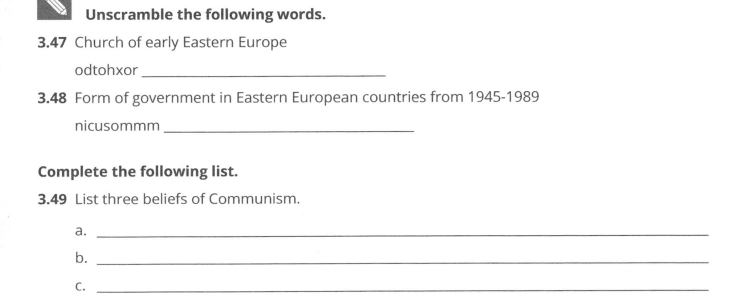

Unscramble the following words.

3.47 Church of early Eastern Europe

odtohxor _____

3.48 Form of government in Eastern European countries from 1945-1989

nicusommm _____

Complete the following list.

3.49 List three beliefs of Communism.

a. _____

b. _____

c. _____

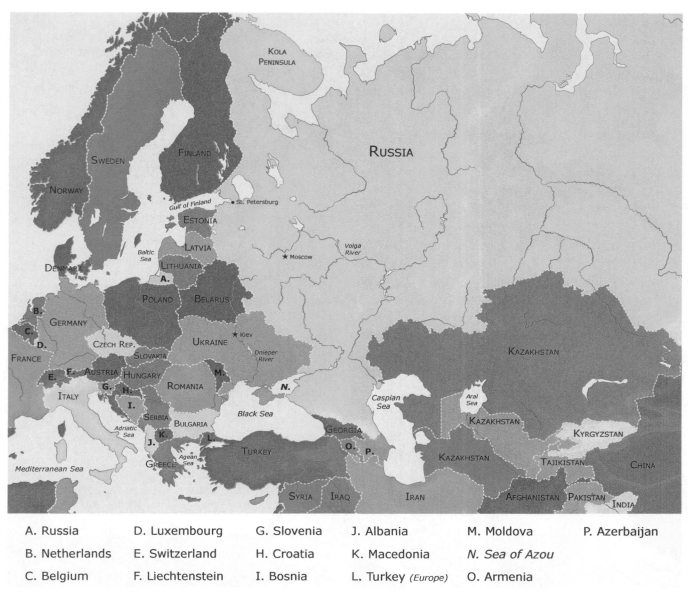

A. Russia	D. Luxembourg	G. Slovenia	J. Albania	M. Moldova	P. Azerbaijan
B. Netherlands	E. Switzerland	H. Croatia	K. Macedonia	N. Sea of Azou	
C. Belgium	F. Liechtenstein	I. Bosnia	L. Turkey (Europe)	O. Armenia	

| Map of Russia and modern Eastern Europe

Communism in Russia. During World War I, V. I. Lenin promised the Russian people plenty of food, no war, and land. These promises were eagerly accepted by the poor of Russia. Russia had been torn by revolution for over ten years. Lenin formed the world's first communist government and withdrew Russia from World War I. Lenin created the Union of Soviet Socialist Republics.

Joseph Stalin succeeded Lenin. Stalin's goal was to build an industrial nation. His plan was called the Five-Year Plan. Under this plan, industry and farmland were controlled by the government. People had few freedoms. Workers received small **wages**. Stalin used secret police to keep citizens in line.

Another Soviet leader, Mikhail Gorbachev, began to give the people in the USSR and in Eastern Europe more freedom in the late 1980s. They used their new freedom to end communism.

Communism was ended in the Soviet Union in 1991. At that same time, the Soviet Union split into fifteen new nations: Russia, Estonia, Latvia, Lithuania, Belarus, Ukraine, Moldova, Georgia, Armenia, Azerbaijan, Turkmenistan, Uzbekistan, Kyrgyzstan, Tajikistan, and Kazakhstan.

Communism in other Eastern European countries. Communism became the form of government for the other Eastern European countries after World War II. Most of these nations became communist while they were occupied by Soviet troops after the war. Only Albania and Yugoslavia became communist without Soviet aid. These nations acted more

independently during the Cold War (1945-1991) than those whose communist leaders owed their power to the USSR.

As soon as the Soviet Union stopped using force to keep communism in place, Eastern European nations began changing their types of governments. With the fall of the Berlin Wall in 1989, East and West Germans formed one united German nation. Hungary, Romania, Bulgaria, Poland and Albania all held free elections. The country of Czechoslovakia divided into two nations: the Czech Republic and Slovakia.

Unfortunately not all of the changes were peaceful. Ethnic violence brought death and destruction to the nation of Yugoslavia. United Nations forces were called in to help stem the violence in the Kosovo area. Yugoslavia has now divided into six separate nations primarily determined by the ethnicity of the people.

Write true or false.

3.50 _____ Lenin and Stalin were Communist leaders of Russia.

3.51 _____ Germany did not reunite after communism ended.

3.52 _____ The Five-Year Plan was Stalin's plan to turn Russia into an industrial nation.

3.53 _____ Under communism, farmland and industry belonged to the government.

3.54 _____ The Soviet Union remained a united power after communism ended.

3.55 _____ Several countries of Eastern Europe kept a communist form of government after 1989.

Review the material in this section in preparation for the Self Test. This Self Test will check your mastery of this particular section as well as your knowledge of the previous sections.

SELF TEST 3

Write true or false (each answer, 2 points).

3.01 _____ Renaissance means *rebirth*, *awakening*.

3.02 _____ Protestants were people who protested corrupt practices of the church.

3.03 _____ Martin Luther, John Calvin, and John Knox opposed the Protestant movement.

3.04 _____ *Reformation* refers to the *reforming of the church*.

3.05 _____ Luther taught that individuals have the freedom to ask forgiveness and receive salvation from God personally.

3.06 _____ The Magna Carta guaranteed rights and privileges to all the people of England.

3.07 _____ The Crusades were journeys to the Holy Land.

3.08 _____ Guilds were formed among merchants of the Middle Ages.

3.09 _____ The Fertile Crescent was the Cradle of Civilization because early civilization began and grew there.

3.010 _____ The Mesopotamians used the wheel and the plow with a metal tip.

Write the letter of the correct answer on each line (each answer, 2 points).

3.011 The Renaissance brought new freedom in _____ .
a. communication b. learning c. economy

3.012 New freedom in learning during the Renaissance has been a foundation for America's freedom of _____ .
a. thought and religion b. communication c. economy

3.013 During the Renaissance, people began to feel that men have the right to _____ .
a. own homes b. govern themselves c. own businesses

3.014 The center of the Industrial Revolution in Western Europe was _____ .
a. Italy b. France c. England

3.015 The Industrial Revolution made it possible for people to buy good products for _____ .
a. low costs b. high costs c. other products

3.016 During the Industrial Revolution, cities became _____ .
a. dirty and overcrowded b. modern c. centers for learning

3.017 The Roman Empire built many _____ .
a. pyramids   b. good roads   c. harbors

3.018 Land distribution during the Middle Ages was called the _____ .
a. villein   b. manor system   c. feudal system

3.019 The Fertile Crescent had sufficient water, good soil, and _____ .
a. cold climate   b. warm climate   c. many rivers

3.020 The books of the Old Testament were written in the language of the _____ people.
a. Hebrew   b. Mesopotamian   c. Roman

Complete these sentences (each answer, 3 points).

3.021 Three sources of energy which made the Industrial Revolution possible were electric

power, coal, and _____ .

3.022 Factories employed adults and _____ .

3.023 Factory laborers worked long, hard hours and received small _____ .

3.024 World War II began in _____ .

3.025 World War I was caused by tensions between countries who wanted more

_____ .

3.026 As a result of World War I, Germany and the Central Powers were reduced in

_____ .

3.027 Greece introduced democratic methods in government and the idea of trial

_____ .

3.028 The Greek Empire was weakened by war between _____ .

3.029 Health and sanitation problems during the Middle Ages included garbage, contaminated

water, and _____ .

3.030 Romans introduced the right of private ownership and the right to be considered innocent

until _____ .

Match these items (each answer, 2 points).

3.031 _____ economic depression, political problems, dictatorships

3.032 _____ Hitler, Stalin, Mussolini

3.033 _____ Five-Year Plan

3.034 _____ Communism

3.035 _____ society with no classes

3.036 _____ United Nations

3.037 _____ East Germany

3.038 _____ West Germany

3.039 _____ city-states

3.040 _____ crusades, interest in learning, prosperity of merchants and townspeople

a. form of government in Eastern Europe from 1945-1989

b. section of Germany governed by Russia following World War II

c. dictators

d. government of Greek Empire

e. brought Middle Ages to a close

f. organization formed after World War II

g. Communist plan which brought less freedom to Russian people

h. section of Germany governed by France, England, and the United States following World War II

i. causes of World War II

j. part of Roman Empire

k. Communist belief

Answer these questions (each answer, 5 points).

3.041 What did Mikhail Gorbachev change and what was the effect in the USSR and Eastern Europe? _____

_____

_____

_____

_____

3.042 How does communism's view of religion differ from a democracy's view of religion?

_____

_____

_____

80/100   SCORE _____   TEACHER _____ _____
                                          initials   date

4. SOUTH AMERICA AND AFRICA

The countries of South America and Africa are part of the modern world. Like past civilizations and European countries, these countries have also experienced change.

Change has brought growth and development. We will review this development of South America and Africa.

Section Objectives

Review these objectives. When you have completed this section, you should be able to:

7.   Name the countries of South America and Africa.

8.   Describe European influence and today's government of South American and African countries.

9.   List resources of South American and African countries.

SOUTH AMERICA

South America is the fourth largest continent in the world. Countries of Western Europe sent explorers and colonists to South America. The development of the South American countries began from colonies. These countries have now developed into independent countries of the modern world.

Six northern South American countries.
The six northern countries of South America are Brazil, Colombia, Venezuela, and the three Guianas: Guyana, Suriname, and French Guiana.

Each of these countries was a colony to a European country. Brazil was a Portuguese colony. Brazil gained its independence in 1824. Today, Brazil is governed by an elected president. Only members of the military may serve as president. Both Colombia and Venezuela were Spanish colonies. A hero in South American history helped both countries win independence. His name was Simón Bolívar. The three Guianas were each owned by a different country. Guyana was owned by Great Britain. Great Britain made Guyana a free territory in 1966. Suriname belonged to the Netherlands. The Netherlands gave Suriname its freedom in 1954. French

| South America

Guiana was used as a colony for prisoners. Today, the prisons are closed. French Guiana is a Department (state) of France.

The people of these six countries are from varied backgrounds. Some are descendants of the Indians. The Indians were the original inhabitants of South America. Some are descendants of the European colonists who settled in that country. Some of the people are descendants of the African slaves. These Slaves were imported from Africa to work for the Europeans during the colonial period. Many of the people are a mixture of Indian, European, or African blood.

Complete the following activities.

4.1   List the six northern South American countries and the European country which colonized them.

South American country	**European country**
a. _____	_____
b. _____	_____
c. _____	_____
d. _____	_____
e. _____	_____
f. _____	_____

4.2   Name the three races of people from whom these South Americans have descended.

a. _____   b. _____

c. _____

Some of the resources produced by these countries make these countries important to the rest of the world. Coffee is a major export of Brazil and Colombia. Oil is exported by Columbia and Venezuela. In fact, oil accounts for 90% of Venezuela's export revenue. Brazil, Guyana and Suriname export bauxite. Aluminum is made from bauxite. French Guiana is famous for its spices. Cayenne pepper, a spicy red pepper, takes its name from a city in French Guiana.

Religion has had and is having an influence in these South American countries. Most of the people are Catholic. The Catholic Church was very important to the people of Western Europe. The people of Western Europe brought this Catholic influence with them to South America. Today, Protestant missionaries are very active in Brazil and Venezuela. Some missionaries live in villages with the Indians. Some missionaries translate the Bible into native languages. Some missionaries use radio programs to tell the people of Jesus Christ and His love.

Write the letter of the resource next to the country from which it comes.
Some answers may be used more than once.

4.3 _____ Brazil

4.4 _____ Colombia

4.5 _____ Venezuela

4.6 _____ Guyana

4.7 _____ Suriname

4.8 _____ French Guiana

a. coffee

b. oil, petroleum

c. bauxite

d. spices

Answer the following questions.

4.9 What are missionaries doing to spread God's Word? _____

_____

_____

_____

4.10 What is bauxite used to make? _____

Seven southern South American countries. The seven southern countries of South America are Ecuador, Peru, Bolivia, Uruguay, Paraguay, Argentina, and Chile.

Each of these countries experienced conquest by Spain. Ecuador, Peru, and Bolivia were home to the highly civilized Inca Indians. The wealth of this civilization attracted the Spanish conquerors. The Spanish invaded Ecuador, Peru, and Bolivia. They were merciless to the Incas. The Inca civilization was destroyed. Its wealth was taken.

The Charrua Indians of Uruguay were hostile to the Spanish settlers. Their fierceness kept European conquerors away for many years. Spain did control Uruguay for a short time. The Indians of Paraguay were peaceful farmers.

Because Paraguay did not have gold, silver or other precious metals, the people were not treated as harshly as those of other conquered areas. Argentina was also controlled by Spain. Spain conquered Chile as well.

Today, each of these countries is an independent nation. Each elects a president to head the government. The mixture of people shows the influence of Spain and other European countries. The majority of the people in Ecuador, Peru, and Bolivia are either Indians or mestizos. Mestizos have both Indian and Spanish blood. 88% of the population of Uruguay is of European descent. Paraguay has the smallest population of all the South American countries. Most of the people are *mestizos*. Most of the population of Argentina is Spanish and Italian. In Chile, most of the people are *mestizos*.

Complete the following sentences.

4.11 All seven of the southern countries of South America were controlled by _____ .

4.12 Ecuador, Peru, and Bolivia were home to the _____ Indians.

4.13 The country which did not have riches to interest Spain was _____ .

4.14 The Indians of Uruguay were very _____ .

4.15 The Indians of Paraguay were _____ .

4.16 Each of these countries is govened by a _____ .

4.17 The president is usually a member of the _____ .

Write the letter of the people group next to the country where they are most common.
Some answers may be used more than once.

4.18 _____ Ecuador, Peru, Bolivia   a. Indian

4.19 _____ Uruguay   b. mestizo

4.20 _____ Paraguay   c. European

4.21 _____ Argentina

4.22 _____ Chile

These countries have begun to develop economically. The chief resource and industry in Ecuador is petroleum. Ecuador also exports agricultural products like bananas, coffee, and cocoa. Peru has vast amounts of mineral resources like copper, gold, and zinc. The country also exports petroleum resources. Near the turn of the millennium, Bolivia discovered large natural gas reserves. The country also exports vast quantities of soybeans and soybean-related products. The major export of Uruguay is cattle along with leather products. Paraguay is the sixth largest exporter of soybeans in the world. The production of oil is important to Argentina. Chile has many mines. Copper, silver, iron, and coal are found throughout the country.

Write the letter of the correct answer on each line.

4.23 The chief resource and industry of Ecuador is _____ .
a. bananas   b. mining   c. cotton

4.24 Peru is the world's second largest producer of _____ .
a. steel   b. metal   c. vanadium

4.25 Vanadium is important in making _____ .
a. steel   b. iron   c. medicine

4.26 Peru has vast natural resources of _____ .
a. gold, silver, and diamonds   b. gold, copper, and zinc   c. gold, silver, and bronze

4.27 Bolivia has recently discovered large reserves of _____ .
a. natural gas   b. oil   c. gold

4.28 The major export of Uruguay is _____ .
a. apples   b. bananas   c. cattle

4.29 Paraguay is the sixth largest exporter of _____ .
a. apples   b. bananas   c. soy beans

4.30 Argentina manufactures _____ .
a. jets and automobiles   b. missiles   c. machinery

4.31 Most of Chile's mining is controlled by large companies in _____ .
a. the United States   b. Spain   c. Chile

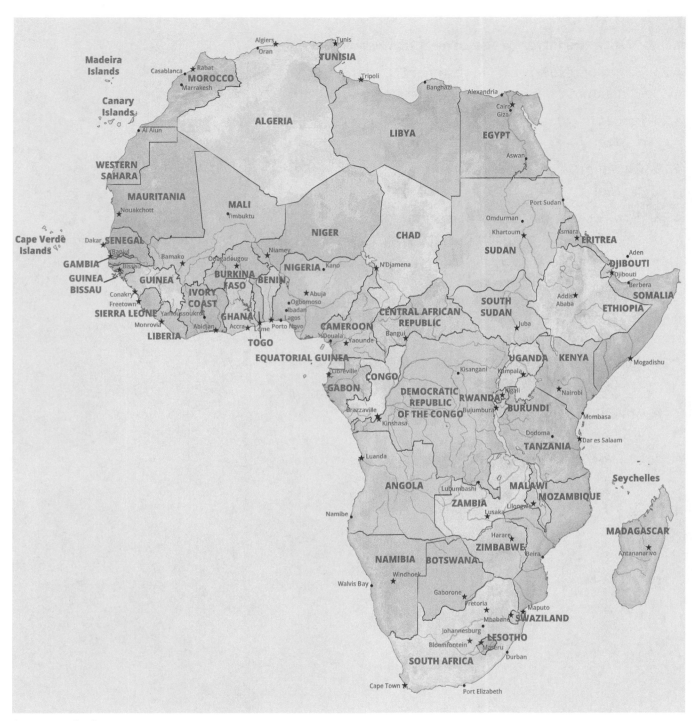

| Map of Africa

AFRICA

Like South America, Africa was also governed by European countries. Today, Africa is independent of Europe. Africa is in the process of growing and developing into a part of the modern world. You will review the names of the African countries and the characteristics of Africa.

Africa, before the coming of the Europeans, was a land with a variety of kingdoms, trading city-states, and small independent tribes. The Europeans came at first to trade, especially for slaves. Eventually, however, they took over all of Africa. They divided it up among themselves, according to what they wanted. African ethnic groups that considered each other enemies suddenly were part of the same nation. This sowed the seeds of many of modern Africa's problems.

The countries of Africa were granted independence primarily in the 1960s. These new nations have suffered deep divisions between the ethnic groups who fought each other for power. When one group did come to power, it formed a one-party government to keep itself in power. When the government became too corrupt or another group become too frustrated with being out of power, the army would take over the government. The constant conflict led to many wars which frequently caused famines. The conflicts were aided by the Cold War between the United States and the Soviet Union. The brutal dictators of Africa could usually gain the support of one of the Super Powers by opposing the other.

The end of the Cold War in 1991 brought free elections to many countries in Africa. But, these nations also owe huge debts. Many have economies ruined by bad government and war. The problems of tribal differences have not been solved. For example, the massacre of 200,000 of the Tutsi people by the Hutus in Rwanda in 1994 was a tribal conflict. The people of Africa need good government and peace before they can prosper from their many resources.

Northern Africa. Locate these countries of northern Africa on the Map of Africa and draw a circle around the name of each country.

Mauritania	Morocco
Western Sahara	Algeria
Tunisia	Libya
Egypt	Sudan
Mali	Niger
Chad	South Sudan

North Africa is dominated by the Sahara Desert. The Sahara is constantly growing due to drought, especially in the Sahel area along its southern edge. The few people who lived in the desert were either nomads or lived on the fertile strips around the Nile River or other water sources. Many of the nations have become wealthy in recent years due to the discovery of oil in their land. Those without oil are desperately poor and need much outside help for their people to survive.

Religion both unites and divides the people. Most of the people are Arabs and use Arabic as their official language. They were converted to Islam by the armies of that religion which swept through in the A.D. 700s. It is still the dominant religion. Much of North Africa is being torn apart by conflicts with Islamic fundamentalists who want to enforce the harsh religious law of Islam on all of the people. Acts of terrorism are common. The governments react by stopping elections, jailing people, and forbidding free speech.

Some of the countries have Muslims in the north and traditional or Christian people in the south. Differences in religion have made their tribal conflicts worse. These countries have had long wars between the two groups that have left the people poor and starving.

Answer or complete the following.

4.32 How do people live in the Sahara Desert? _____

_____

4.33 What two things do the people of Africa need before they can prosper?

_____ .

4.34 Why have many nations had free elections in the 1990s?

_____ .

4.35 What is the main religion of North Africa? _____ .

4.36 What group of people want to use Islam's religious law as the law of their countries?

_____ .

4.37 List the northern countries of Africa.

a. _____   b. _____

c. _____   d. _____

e. _____   f. _____

g. _____   h. _____

i. _____   j. _____

k. _____   l. _____

Central Africa. Locate these central African countries on the Map of Africa and draw a box around the name of each country.

Senegal	The Gambia
Guinea-Bissau	Guinea
Burkina Faso	Sierra Leone
Liberia	Cote d'Ivoire
Ghana	Togo
Benin	Nigeria
Cameroon	Equatorial Guinea
Central African	Democratic Republic of
Republic	the Congo
Congo	Gabon
Rwanda	Burundi
Tanzania	Uganda
Kenya	Ethiopia
Eritrea	Somalia
Djibouti	

Much of central Africa is covered by tropical rainforests surrounded by savanna. The Congo River Basin covers much of the central interior. The people are from many different ethnic groups. They have different religions. They tend to fight rather than co-operate with each other.

It was from central Africa that the nations of Europe took most of their slaves. They got the slaves by trading with the powerful African tribes who captured people from other tribes and sold them. Britain took the lead in ending this horrible trade in the 1800s. By then, the Europeans were taking over the areas with which they traded in order to get ivory, timber, rubber, gold, and other resources.

Today, many of these nations are very poor in spite of their many resources. This is usually the result of bad government. Until 1990, most of the governments either had only one ruling party or were run by the military. Both of these tended to be corrupt. Much of the governments' money was stolen. Also, many of the nations tried communism or socialism. Under these economic systems the government ran many or all of the businesses. The government did not run the businesses well. Money was wasted on bad decisions and paying unnecessary people. Many African nations are trying to reduce government control to let people run their own businesses and farms.

 Answer or complete the following.

4.38 Place an *X* in front of the twenty-seven central African countries.

a.	_____	Senegal	s.	_____	Liberia
b.	_____	The Gambia	t.	_____	Mesopotamia
c.	_____	Peru	u.	_____	Greece
d.	_____	Guinea	v.	_____	Ivory Coast
e.	_____	Guinea-Bissau	w.	_____	Ghana
f.	_____	Guyana	x.	_____	Togo
g.	_____	Burkina Faso	y.	_____	Benin
h.	_____	Sierra Leone	z.	_____	Nigeria
i.	_____	Cameroon	aa.	_____	France
j.	_____	Iran	bb.	_____	Rwanda
k.	_____	Suriname	cc.	_____	Burundi
l.	_____	Equatorial Guinea	dd.	_____	Tanzania
m.	_____	Central African Republic	ee.	_____	Uganda
n.	_____	Gabon	ff.	_____	Kenya
o.	_____	Congo	gg.	_____	Ethiopia
p.	_____	D.R. of the Congo	hh.	_____	Somalia
q.	_____	Bahamas	ii.	_____	Djibouti
r.	_____	Eritrea	jj.	_____	Ecuador

4.39 How did the Europeans get African slaves? _____

_____

4.40 Central Africa is covered mostly by _____

_____ .

4.41 Until 1990, most African nations were governed by _____ .

Southern Africa. Locate each of these countries from southern Africa on the Map of Africa and draw a line beneath the name of each.

Angola	Madagascar
South Africa	Namibia
Swaziland	Lesotho
Botswana	Zambia
Malawi	Zimbabwe
Mozambique	

Southern Africa is more temperate than the north. It is further from the equator and it sits on the Southern Plateau where temperatures are cooler. The soil is good for crops and cattle except for the Namib and Kalahari Deserts. The area is rich in a wide variety of resources including gold, diamonds, copper, iron, and many others. The people include a number of Black African tribes as well as the descendants of White settlers and people of mixed race called Coloureds.

Conflict between the White settlers and the native people has marked southern Africa's modern history. Swaziland, Lesotho, and Botswana were all African kingdoms which became British Protectorates to prevent the settlers from taking their land. The Whites in Zimbabwe and South Africa set up special rules that gave them all the power, money, and best jobs. This was called apartheid in South Africa. Namibia was conquered and held by South Africa from World War II until 1990. The other countries, which did not have large numbers of White settlers, fought among themselves, often with Soviet aid. Angola, for example, had Cuban soldiers helping the communist government stay in power.

Free elections have been held in many of these countries since 1990. Many are suffering the effects of long terrorist fights between different groups. Many suffered famine and ruined economies. The different groups still do not trust each other. The governments are all new and have no experience with solving these problems. Again peace and good government are needed.

 Complete the following.

4.42 Rewrite the list of southern African countries in alphabetical order.

Zambia	Lesotho	Angola
Zimbabwe	Malawi	Swaziland
Namibia	Mozambique	Botswana
South Africa	Madagascar	

a. _____   b. _____

c. _____   d. _____

e. _____   f. _____

g. _____   h. _____

i. _____   j. _____

k. _____

Match the following items.

4.43 _____ White settlers and Black Africans

4.44 _____ South Africa's system of separating races

4.45 _____ African kingdoms that became British Protectorates

4.46 _____ What Africa needs to become prosperous and modern

4.47 _____ Resources of sothern Africa

a. Swaziland, Lethoso

b. Main groups in conflict separating races in southern Africa

c. Peace and good British Protectorates government

d. Gold, diamonds, copper, prosperous and modern fertile land

e. Apartheid

Before you take this last Self Test, you may want to do one or more of the following self checks.

1. _____ Read the objectives. See if you can do them.
2. _____ Restudy the material related to any objectives that you cannot do.
3. _____ Use the **SQ3R** study procedure to review the material:
   a. **S**can the sections.
   b. **Q**uestion yourself.
   c. **R**ead to answer your questions.
   d. **R**ecite the answers to yourself.
   e. **R**eview areas you did not understand.
4. _____ Review all vocabulary, activities, and Self Tests, writing a correct answer for every wrong answer.

SELF TEST 4

Write true or false (each answer, 2 points).

4.01 _____ The people of northern South America have descended from either Indian, European, or African people.

4.02 _____ Brazil is the world's largest coffee producer.

4.03 _____ Colombia also produces coffee.

4.04 _____ French Guiana is known for its spices.

4.05 _____ Venezuela and Colombia produce oil.

4.06 _____ South American presidents are usually members of the military.

4.07 _____ Three sources of energy which made the Industrial Revolution possible were electric power, coal, and water power.

4.08 _____ Children could not work in the factories during the Industrial Revolution.

4.09 _____ World War II began in 1914.

4.010 _____ Economic depression, political problems, and dictatorships were the main causes of World War II.

Write the letter of the correct answer on each line (each answer, 2 points).

4.011 All seven of the southern countries of South America were controlled by _____ .
a. England   b. Portugal   c. Spain

4.012 Ecuador, Peru, and Bolivia were home to the _____ Indians.
a. Aztec   b. Inca   c. American

4.013 The people in _____ were not treated as harshly by the Spanish because the country did not have gold or silver deposits.
a. Paraguay   b. Peru   c. French Guiana

4.014 Large reserves of natural gas have recently been discovered in _____ .
a. Chile   b. Brazil   c. Bolivia

4.015 People in South America with both Indian and Spanish blood are called _____ .
a. mestizo   b. Spaniards   c. mulatto

4.016 The Spanish destroyed the _____ civilization which was found.
a. Aztec   b. Incan   c. Charruah

4.017 Merchandise brought back from the Crusades included jewels, perfume, and _____ .
a. diamonds   b. gold   c. silk

4.018 Martin Luther, John Calvin, and John Knox were _____ .
a. Protestants   b. Catholic priests   c. crusaders

4.019 An important document signed during the Renaissance was the _____ .
a. Declaration of Independence
b. Magna Carta
c. Mayflower Contract

4.020 The great changes which occurred in industry were called _____ .
a. the Industrial Revolution   b. urbanization   c. war on poverty

Complete these sentences (each answer, 3 points).

4.021 The main religion of North Africa is _____ .

4.022 The natural feature which dominates northern Africa is the _____ .

4.023 Before 1990, most African nations had one of two forms of government. List both.

a. _____   b. _____

4.024 The Europeans especially wanted to trade for _____ before the 1800s.

4.025 What two things do the people of Africa need to become prosperous?

a. _____   b. _____

4.026 Aluminum is made from _____ .

4.027 *Renaissance* means _____ .

4.028 The period following the fall of the Roman Empire was called the _____ .

4.029 During the Middle Ages, merchants formed _____ .

4.030 Journeys made to the Holy Land during the Middle Ages were called _____ .

Match these items (each answer, 2 points).

4.031 _____ Brazil, Colombia, Venezuela

4.032 _____ gold, diamonds

4.033 _____ Egypt, Israel, Mesopotamia

4.034 _____ Chile, Argentine, Uruguay

4.035 _____ Sudan, Egypt, Morocco, South Sudan

4.036 _____ Hebrews

4.037 _____ Nigeria, Cameroon, Ethiopia

4.038 _____ Athens, Sparta

4.039 _____ Angola, Nambia, Zimbabwe

4.040 _____ slaves, common citizens, equestrians, aristocrats

a. countries of northern Africa

b. ruler of Egypt

c. countries of northern South America

d. population areas of Fertile Crescent

e. countries of central Africa

f. resources of southern Africa

g. Greek city-states

h. classes of people in Roman Empire

i. God's chosen people

j. countries of southern South America

k. countries of southern Africa

Answer these questions (each answer, 5 points).

4.041 How did Vasco da Gama help begin European settlement in southern Africa?

_____

_____

_____

_____

4.042 What were three of the negative effects of the Industrial Revolution?

_____

_____

_____

$\frac{85}{106}$ SCORE _____ TEACHER _____ _____

initials   date

Before taking the LIFEPAC Test, you may want to do one or more of these self checks.

1. _____ Read the objectives. See if you can do them.
2. _____ Restudy the material related to any objectives that you cannot do.
3. _____ Use the **SQ3R** study procedure to review the material.
4. _____ Review activities, Self Tests, and LIFEPAC vocabulary words.
5. _____ Restudy areas of weakness indicated by the last Self Test.

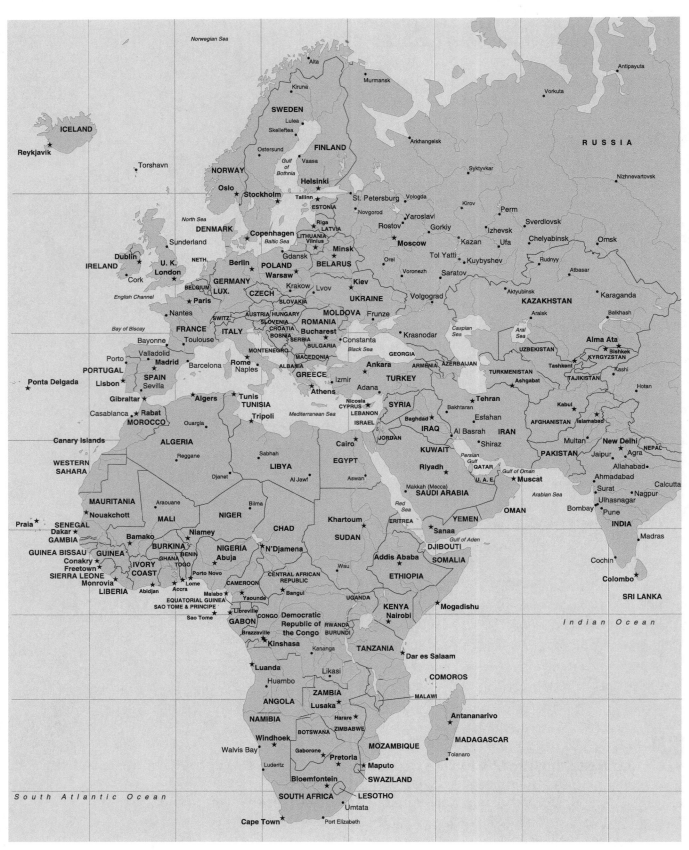

| Europe, Africa and Western Asia